This book belongs to:

_____

Contact info:

Phone: _____

Cell: _____

Text: _____

Email: _____

My Passwords
© *2014 V.B. Blake*

All Rights Reserved

ISBN-13: 978-1503244269
ISBN-10: 1503244261

Passwords

Tips on choosing a password:

- choose at least 6 characters - the longer the password the stronger it is
- the more complex and obscure your password is the more secure it is
- use upper and lower case characters
- use symbols
- use a selection of letters or a misspelled phrase, e.g., jElL()dHo()T#rs*Me (jello shooters for me)
- pick unrelated words, e.g., concretemitts
- choose a phrase that's easy for you to remember then using the first letters of that phrase substitute various characters, e.g., "Best TV Series Ever: Game of Thrones"; becomes: btvsegot; becomes: b:^$3g0+
- stay away from obvious words, such as pet's name, birthdays, etc. - they can be found easily on social media sites like Facebook

Frequency of password changes:

- change your email accounts passwords frequently, every 90 days or so
- hackers with access to your email account can retrieve passwords from other sites using "forgot your password?"
- if a website has been compromised, do not change your password until the security breach has been patched and the site is again safe; changing a password before patching may not have an impact or could potentially expose your new password
- consider using a 'two-factor authorization', also known as 'second factor' or 'login verification'

Site Name: _____ http://_____
User Name: _____ Email: _____
Password: _____ Phone: _____
                                      Acct. #: _____
Email Log In: _____
Security Questions: _____
_____
Reminders: _____
_____

Site Name: _____ http://_____
User Name: _____ Email: _____
Password: _____ Phone: _____
                                      Acct. #: _____
Email Log In: _____
Security Questions: _____
_____
Reminders: _____
_____

Site Name: _____ http://_____
User Name: _____ Email: _____
Password: _____ Phone: _____
                                      Acct. #: _____
Email Log In: _____
Security Questions: _____
_____
Reminders: _____
_____

Site Name: _____ http://_____
User Name: _____ Email: _____
Password: _____ Phone: _____
                                      Acct. #: _____
Email Log In: _____
Security Questions: _____
_____
Reminders: _____
_____

Site Name: _____ http://_____
User Name: _____ Email: _____
Password: _____ Phone: _____
                                      Acct. #: _____
Email Log In: _____
Security Questions: _____
_____
Reminders: _____
_____

Aa

Site Name: _____ http://_____
User Name: _____ Email: _____
Password: _____ Phone: _____
Acct. #: _____

Email Log In: _____
Security Questions: _____
_____

Reminders: _____
_____

Site Name: _____ http://_____
User Name: _____ Email: _____
Password: _____ Phone: _____
Acct. #: _____

Email Log In: _____
Security Questions: _____
_____

Reminders: _____
_____

Site Name: _____ http://_____
User Name: _____ Email: _____
Password: _____ Phone: _____
Acct. #: _____

Email Log In: _____
Security Questions: _____
_____

Reminders: _____
_____

Site Name: _____ http://_____
User Name: _____ Email: _____
Password: _____ Phone: _____
Acct. #: _____

Email Log In: _____
Security Questions: _____
_____

Reminders: _____
_____

Site Name: _____ http://_____
User Name: _____ Email: _____
Password: _____ Phone: _____
Acct. #: _____

Email Log In: _____
Security Questions: _____
_____

Reminders: _____

Aa

Site Name: _____ http://_____
User Name: _____ Email: _____
Password: _____ Phone: _____
                                     Acct. #: _____

Email Log In: _____
Security Questions: _____
_____

Reminders: _____
_____

Site Name: _____ http://_____
User Name: _____ Email: _____
Password: _____ Phone: _____
                                     Acct. #: _____

Email Log In: _____
Security Questions: _____
_____

Reminders: _____
_____

Site Name: _____ http://_____
User Name: _____ Email: _____
Password: _____ Phone: _____
                                     Acct. #: _____

Email Log In: _____
Security Questions: _____
_____

Reminders: _____
_____

Site Name: _____ http://_____
User Name: _____ Email: _____
Password: _____ Phone: _____
                                     Acct. #: _____

Email Log In: _____
Security Questions: _____
_____

Reminders: _____
_____

Site Name: _____ http://_____
User Name: _____ Email: _____
Password: _____ Phone: _____
                                     Acct. #: _____

Email Log In: _____
Security Questions: _____
_____

Reminders: _____
_____

Aa

Site Name: _____ http://_____
User Name: _____ Email: _____
Password: _____ Phone: _____
_____ Acct. #: _____
Email Log In: _____
Security Questions: _____
_____
Reminders: _____
_____

Site Name: _____ http://_____
User Name: _____ Email: _____
Password: _____ Phone: _____
_____ Acct. #: _____
Email Log In: _____
Security Questions: _____
_____
Reminders: _____
_____

Site Name: _____ http://_____
User Name: _____ Email: _____
Password: _____ Phone: _____
_____ Acct. #: _____
Email Log In: _____
Security Questions: _____
_____
Reminders: _____
_____

Site Name: _____ http://_____
User Name: _____ Email: _____
Password: _____ Phone: _____
_____ Acct. #: _____
Email Log In: _____
Security Questions: _____
_____
Reminders: _____
_____

Site Name: _____ http://_____
User Name: _____ Email: _____
Password: _____ Phone: _____
_____ Acct. #: _____
Email Log In: _____
Security Questions: _____
_____
Reminders: _____
_____

Bb

Site Name: _____ http://_____
User Name: _____ Email: _____
Password: _____ Phone: _____
                                      Acct. #: _____
Email Log In: _____
Security Questions: _____
_____
Reminders: _____
_____

Site Name: _____ http://_____
User Name: _____ Email: _____
Password: _____ Phone: _____
                                      Acct. #: _____
Email Log In: _____
Security Questions: _____
_____
Reminders: _____
_____

Site Name: _____ http://_____
User Name: _____ Email: _____
Password: _____ Phone: _____
                                      Acct. #: _____
Email Log In: _____
Security Questions: _____
_____
Reminders: _____
_____

Site Name: _____ http://_____
User Name: _____ Email: _____
Password: _____ Phone: _____
                                      Acct. #: _____
Email Log In: _____
Security Questions: _____
_____
Reminders: _____
_____

Site Name: _____ http://_____
User Name: _____ Email: _____
Password: _____ Phone: _____
                                      Acct. #: _____
Email Log In: _____
Security Questions: _____
_____
Reminders: _____
_____

Bb

Site Name: _____ http://_____
User Name: _____ Email: _____
Password: _____ Phone: _____
                                    Acct. #: _____
Email Log In: _____
Security Questions: _____
_____
Reminders: _____
_____

Site Name: _____ http://_____
User Name: _____ Email: _____
Password: _____ Phone: _____
                                    Acct. #: _____
Email Log In: _____
Security Questions: _____
_____
Reminders: _____
_____

Site Name: _____ http://_____
User Name: _____ Email: _____
Password: _____ Phone: _____
                                    Acct. #: _____
Email Log In: _____
Security Questions: _____
_____
Reminders: _____
_____

Site Name: _____ http://_____
User Name: _____ Email: _____
Password: _____ Phone: _____
                                    Acct. #: _____
Email Log In: _____
Security Questions: _____
_____
Reminders: _____
_____

Site Name: _____ http://_____
User Name: _____ Email: _____
Password: _____ Phone: _____
                                    Acct. #: _____
Email Log In: _____
Security Questions: _____
_____
Reminders: _____
_____

Bb

Site Name: _____ http://_____
User Name: _____ Email: _____
Password: _____ Phone: _____
_____ Acct. #: _____
Email Log In: _____
Security Questions: _____
_____
Reminders: _____
_____

Site Name: _____ http://_____
User Name: _____ Email: _____
Password: _____ Phone: _____
_____ Acct. #: _____
Email Log In: _____
Security Questions: _____
_____
Reminders: _____
_____

Site Name: _____ http://_____
User Name: _____ Email: _____
Password: _____ Phone: _____
_____ Acct. #: _____
Email Log In: _____
Security Questions: _____
_____
Reminders: _____
_____

Site Name: _____ http://_____
User Name: _____ Email: _____
Password: _____ Phone: _____
_____ Acct. #: _____
Email Log In: _____
Security Questions: _____
_____
Reminders: _____
_____

Site Name: _____ http://_____
User Name: _____ Email: _____
Password: _____ Phone: _____
_____ Acct. #: _____
Email Log In: _____
Security Questions: _____
_____
Reminders: _____
_____

Bb

Site Name: _____ http:// _____
User Name: _____ Email: _____
Password: _____ Phone: _____
                                                  Acct. #: _____
Email Log In: _____
Security Questions: _____
_____
Reminders: _____
_____

Site Name: _____ http:// _____
User Name: _____ Email: _____
Password: _____ Phone: _____
                                                  Acct. #: _____
Email Log In: _____
Security Questions: _____
_____
Reminders: _____
_____

Site Name: _____ http:// _____
User Name: _____ Email: _____
Password: _____ Phone: _____
                                                  Acct. #: _____
Email Log In: _____
Security Questions: _____
_____
Reminders: _____
_____

Site Name: _____ http:// _____
User Name: _____ Email: _____
Password: _____ Phone: _____
                                                  Acct. #: _____
Email Log In: _____
Security Questions: _____
_____
Reminders: _____
_____

Site Name: _____ http:// _____
User Name: _____ Email: _____
Password: _____ Phone: _____
                                                  Acct. #: _____
Email Log In: _____
Security Questions: _____
_____
Reminders: _____
_____

Cc

Site Name: _____ http://_____
User Name: _____ Email: _____
Password: _____ Phone: _____
                                     Acct. #: _____
Email Log In: _____
Security Questions: _____
_____

Reminders: _____
_____

Site Name: _____ http://_____
User Name: _____ Email: _____
Password: _____ Phone: _____
                                     Acct. #: _____
Email Log In: _____
Security Questions: _____
_____

Reminders: _____
_____

Site Name: _____ http://_____
User Name: _____ Email: _____
Password: _____ Phone: _____
                                     Acct. #: _____
Email Log In: _____
Security Questions: _____
_____

Reminders: _____
_____

Site Name: _____ http://_____
User Name: _____ Email: _____
Password: _____ Phone: _____
                                     Acct. #: _____
Email Log In: _____
Security Questions: _____
_____

Reminders: _____
_____

Site Name: _____ http://_____
User Name: _____ Email: _____
Password: _____ Phone: _____
                                     Acct. #: _____
Email Log In: _____
Security Questions: _____
_____

Reminders: _____
_____

Cc

Site Name: _____ http://_____
User Name: _____ Email: _____
Password: _____ Phone: _____
                                     Acct. #: _____
Email Log In: _____
Security Questions: _____
_____
Reminders: _____
_____

Site Name: _____ http://_____
User Name: _____ Email: _____
Password: _____ Phone: _____
                                     Acct. #: _____
Email Log In: _____
Security Questions: _____
_____
Reminders: _____
_____

Site Name: _____ http://_____
User Name: _____ Email: _____
Password: _____ Phone: _____
                                     Acct. #: _____
Email Log In: _____
Security Questions: _____
_____
Reminders: _____
_____

Site Name: _____ http://_____
User Name: _____ Email: _____
Password: _____ Phone: _____
                                     Acct. #: _____
Email Log In: _____
Security Questions: _____
_____
Reminders: _____
_____

Site Name: _____ http://_____
User Name: _____ Email: _____
Password: _____ Phone: _____
                                     Acct. #: _____
Email Log In: _____
Security Questions: _____
_____
Reminders: _____
_____

Cc

Site Name: _____ http://_____
User Name: _____ Email: _____
Password: _____ Phone: _____
                                      Acct. #: _____
Email Log In: _____
Security Questions: _____
_____
Reminders: _____
_____

Site Name: _____ http://_____
User Name: _____ Email: _____
Password: _____ Phone: _____
                                      Acct. #: _____
Email Log In: _____
Security Questions: _____
_____
Reminders: _____
_____

Site Name: _____ http://_____
User Name: _____ Email: _____
Password: _____ Phone: _____
                                      Acct. #: _____
Email Log In: _____
Security Questions: _____
_____
Reminders: _____
_____

Site Name: _____ http://_____
User Name: _____ Email: _____
Password: _____ Phone: _____
                                      Acct. #: _____
Email Log In: _____
Security Questions: _____
_____
Reminders: _____
_____

Site Name: _____ http://_____
User Name: _____ Email: _____
Password: _____ Phone: _____
                                      Acct. #: _____
Email Log In: _____
Security Questions: _____
_____
Reminders: _____
_____

Cc

Site Name: _____ http://_____
User Name: _____ Email: _____
Password: _____ Phone: _____
                                                Acct. #: _____
Email Log In: _____
Security Questions: _____
_____

Reminders: _____
_____

Site Name: _____ http://_____
User Name: _____ Email: _____
Password: _____ Phone: _____
                                                Acct. #: _____
Email Log In: _____
Security Questions: _____
_____

Reminders: _____
_____

Site Name: _____ http://_____
User Name: _____ Email: _____
Password: _____ Phone: _____
                                                Acct. #: _____
Email Log In: _____
Security Questions: _____
_____

Reminders: _____
_____

Site Name: _____ http://_____
User Name: _____ Email: _____
Password: _____ Phone: _____
                                                Acct. #: _____
Email Log In: _____
Security Questions: _____
_____

Reminders: _____
_____

Site Name: _____ http://_____
User Name: _____ Email: _____
Password: _____ Phone: _____
                                                Acct. #: _____
Email Log In: _____
Security Questions: _____
_____

Reminders: _____
_____

Dd

Site Name: _____ http://_____
User Name: _____ Email: _____
Password: _____ Phone: _____
Acct. #: _____

Email Log In: _____
Security Questions: _____
_____

Reminders: _____
_____

Site Name: _____ http://_____
User Name: _____ Email: _____
Password: _____ Phone: _____
Acct. #: _____

Email Log In: _____
Security Questions: _____
_____

Reminders: _____
_____

Site Name: _____ http://_____
User Name: _____ Email: _____
Password: _____ Phone: _____
Acct. #: _____

Email Log In: _____
Security Questions: _____
_____

Reminders: _____
_____

Site Name: _____ http://_____
User Name: _____ Email: _____
Password: _____ Phone: _____
Acct. #: _____

Email Log In: _____
Security Questions: _____
_____

Reminders: _____
_____

Site Name: _____ http://_____
User Name: _____ Email: _____
Password: _____ Phone: _____
Acct. #: _____

Email Log In: _____
Security Questions: _____
_____

Reminders: _____
_____

Dd

Site Name: _____ http://_____
User Name: _____ Email: _____
Password: _____ Phone: _____
                                        Acct. #: _____

Email Log In: _____
Security Questions: _____
_____

Reminders: _____
_____

Site Name: _____ http://_____
User Name: _____ Email: _____
Password: _____ Phone: _____
                                        Acct. #: _____

Email Log In: _____
Security Questions: _____
_____

Reminders: _____
_____

Site Name: _____ http://_____
User Name: _____ Email: _____
Password: _____ Phone: _____
                                        Acct. #: _____

Email Log In: _____
Security Questions: _____
_____

Reminders: _____
_____

Site Name: _____ http://_____
User Name: _____ Email: _____
Password: _____ Phone: _____
                                        Acct. #: _____

Email Log In: _____
Security Questions: _____
_____

Reminders: _____
_____

Site Name: _____ http://_____
User Name: _____ Email: _____
Password: _____ Phone: _____
                                        Acct. #: _____

Email Log In: _____
Security Questions: _____
_____

Reminders: _____
_____

Dd

Site Name: _____ http:// _____
User Name: _____ Email: _____
Password: _____ Phone: _____
                                   Acct. #: _____
Email Log In: _____
Security Questions: _____
_____
Reminders: _____
_____

Site Name: _____ http:// _____
User Name: _____ Email: _____
Password: _____ Phone: _____
                                   Acct. #: _____
Email Log In: _____
Security Questions: _____
_____
Reminders: _____
_____

Site Name: _____ http:// _____
User Name: _____ Email: _____
Password: _____ Phone: _____
                                   Acct. #: _____
Email Log In: _____
Security Questions: _____
_____
Reminders: _____
_____

Site Name: _____ http:// _____
User Name: _____ Email: _____
Password: _____ Phone: _____
                                   Acct. #: _____
Email Log In: _____
Security Questions: _____
_____
Reminders: _____
_____

Site Name: _____ http:// _____
User Name: _____ Email: _____
Password: _____ Phone: _____
                                   Acct. #: _____
Email Log In: _____
Security Questions: _____
_____
Reminders: _____
_____

Dd

Site Name: _____ http://_____
User Name: _____ Email: _____
Password: _____ Phone: _____
_____ Acct. #: _____
Email Log In: _____
Security Questions: _____
_____
Reminders: _____
_____

Site Name: _____ http://_____
User Name: _____ Email: _____
Password: _____ Phone: _____
_____ Acct. #: _____
Email Log In: _____
Security Questions: _____
_____
Reminders: _____
_____

Site Name: _____ http://_____
User Name: _____ Email: _____
Password: _____ Phone: _____
_____ Acct. #: _____
Email Log In: _____
Security Questions: _____
_____
Reminders: _____
_____

Site Name: _____ http://_____
User Name: _____ Email: _____
Password: _____ Phone: _____
_____ Acct. #: _____
Email Log In: _____
Security Questions: _____
_____
Reminders: _____
_____

Site Name: _____ http://_____
User Name: _____ Email: _____
Password: _____ Phone: _____
_____ Acct. #: _____
Email Log In: _____
Security Questions: _____
_____
Reminders: _____
_____

Site Name: _____ http://_____
User Name: _____ Email: _____
Password: _____ Phone: _____
                                      Acct. #: _____
Email Log In: _____
Security Questions: _____
_____
Reminders: _____
_____

Site Name: _____ http://_____
User Name: _____ Email: _____
Password: _____ Phone: _____
                                      Acct. #: _____
Email Log In: _____
Security Questions: _____
_____
Reminders: _____
_____

Site Name: _____ http://_____
User Name: _____ Email: _____
Password: _____ Phone: _____
                                      Acct. #: _____
Email Log In: _____
Security Questions: _____
_____
Reminders: _____
_____

Site Name: _____ http://_____
User Name: _____ Email: _____
Password: _____ Phone: _____
                                      Acct. #: _____
Email Log In: _____
Security Questions: _____
_____
Reminders: _____
_____

Site Name: _____ http://_____
User Name: _____ Email: _____
Password: _____ Phone: _____
                                      Acct. #: _____
Email Log In: _____
Security Questions: _____
_____
Reminders: _____
_____

Ee

Site Name: _____ http://_____
User Name: _____ Email: _____
Password: _____ Phone: _____
                                   Acct. #: _____
Email Log In: _____
Security Questions: _____
_____

Reminders: _____
_____

Site Name: _____ http://_____
User Name: _____ Email: _____
Password: _____ Phone: _____
                                   Acct. #: _____
Email Log In: _____
Security Questions: _____
_____

Reminders: _____
_____

Site Name: _____ http://_____
User Name: _____ Email: _____
Password: _____ Phone: _____
                                   Acct. #: _____
Email Log In: _____
Security Questions: _____
_____

Reminders: _____
_____

Site Name: _____ http://_____
User Name: _____ Email: _____
Password: _____ Phone: _____
                                   Acct. #: _____
Email Log In: _____
Security Questions: _____
_____

Reminders: _____
_____

Site Name: _____ http://_____
User Name: _____ Email: _____
Password: _____ Phone: _____
                                   Acct. #: _____
Email Log In: _____
Security Questions: _____
_____

Reminders: _____
_____

Ee

Site Name: _____ http://_____
User Name: _____ Email: _____
Password: _____ Phone: _____
                                      Acct. #: _____
Email Log In: _____
Security Questions: _____
_____
Reminders: _____
_____

Site Name: _____ http://_____
User Name: _____ Email: _____
Password: _____ Phone: _____
                                      Acct. #: _____
Email Log In: _____
Security Questions: _____
_____
Reminders: _____
_____

Site Name: _____ http://_____
User Name: _____ Email: _____
Password: _____ Phone: _____
                                      Acct. #: _____
Email Log In: _____
Security Questions: _____
_____
Reminders: _____
_____

Site Name: _____ http://_____
User Name: _____ Email: _____
Password: _____ Phone: _____
                                      Acct. #: _____
Email Log In: _____
Security Questions: _____
_____
Reminders: _____
_____

Site Name: _____ http://_____
User Name: _____ Email: _____
Password: _____ Phone: _____
                                      Acct. #: _____
Email Log In: _____
Security Questions: _____
_____
Reminders: _____
_____

Ee

Site Name: _____ http://_____
User Name: _____ Email: _____
Password: _____ Phone: _____
                                     Acct. #: _____
Email Log In: _____
Security Questions: _____
_____
Reminders: _____
_____

Site Name: _____ http://_____
User Name: _____ Email: _____
Password: _____ Phone: _____
                                     Acct. #: _____
Email Log In: _____
Security Questions: _____
_____
Reminders: _____
_____

Site Name: _____ http://_____
User Name: _____ Email: _____
Password: _____ Phone: _____
                                     Acct. #: _____
Email Log In: _____
Security Questions: _____
_____
Reminders: _____
_____

Site Name: _____ http://_____
User Name: _____ Email: _____
Password: _____ Phone: _____
                                     Acct. #: _____
Email Log In: _____
Security Questions: _____
_____
Reminders: _____
_____

Site Name: _____ http://_____
User Name: _____ Email: _____
Password: _____ Phone: _____
                                     Acct. #: _____
Email Log In: _____
Security Questions: _____
_____
Reminders: _____
_____

Ff

Site Name: _____ http://_____

User Name: _____ Email: _____

Password: _____ Phone: _____

Acct. #: _____

Email Log In: _____

Security Questions: _____

_____

Reminders: _____

_____

Site Name: _____ http://_____

User Name: _____ Email: _____

Password: _____ Phone: _____

Acct. #: _____

Email Log In: _____

Security Questions: _____

_____

Reminders: _____

_____

Site Name: _____ http://_____

User Name: _____ Email: _____

Password: _____ Phone: _____

Acct. #: _____

Email Log In: _____

Security Questions: _____

_____

Reminders: _____

_____

Site Name: _____ http://_____

User Name: _____ Email: _____

Password: _____ Phone: _____

Acct. #: _____

Email Log In: _____

Security Questions: _____

_____

Reminders: _____

_____

Site Name: _____ http://_____

User Name: _____ Email: _____

Password: _____ Phone: _____

Acct. #: _____

Email Log In: _____

Security Questions: _____

_____

Reminders: _____

_____

Ff

Site Name: _____ http://_____
User Name: _____ Email: _____
Password: _____ Phone: _____
                                     Acct. #: _____

Email Log In: _____
Security Questions: _____
_____

Reminders: _____
_____

Site Name: _____ http://_____
User Name: _____ Email: _____
Password: _____ Phone: _____
                                     Acct. #: _____

Email Log In: _____
Security Questions: _____
_____

Reminders: _____
_____

Site Name: _____ http://_____
User Name: _____ Email: _____
Password: _____ Phone: _____
                                     Acct. #: _____

Email Log In: _____
Security Questions: _____
_____

Reminders: _____
_____

Site Name: _____ http://_____
User Name: _____ Email: _____
Password: _____ Phone: _____
                                     Acct. #: _____

Email Log In: _____
Security Questions: _____
_____

Reminders: _____
_____

Site Name: _____ http://_____
User Name: _____ Email: _____
Password: _____ Phone: _____
                                     Acct. #: _____

Email Log In: _____
Security Questions: _____
_____

Reminders: _____
_____

Ff

Site Name: _____ http://_____
User Name: _____ Email: _____
Password: _____ Phone: _____
                                     Acct. #: _____
Email Log In: _____
Security Questions: _____
_____
Reminders: _____
_____

Site Name: _____ http://_____
User Name: _____ Email: _____
Password: _____ Phone: _____
                                     Acct. #: _____
Email Log In: _____
Security Questions: _____
_____
Reminders: _____
_____

Site Name: _____ http://_____
User Name: _____ Email: _____
Password: _____ Phone: _____
                                     Acct. #: _____
Email Log In: _____
Security Questions: _____
_____
Reminders: _____
_____

Site Name: _____ http://_____
User Name: _____ Email: _____
Password: _____ Phone: _____
                                     Acct. #: _____
Email Log In: _____
Security Questions: _____
_____
Reminders: _____
_____

Site Name: _____ http://_____
User Name: _____ Email: _____
Password: _____ Phone: _____
                                     Acct. #: _____
Email Log In: _____
Security Questions: _____
_____
Reminders: _____
_____

Ff

Site Name: _____ http://_____
User Name: _____ Email: _____
Password: _____ Phone: _____
                                   Acct. #: _____
Email Log In: _____
Security Questions: _____
_____

Reminders: _____
_____

Site Name: _____ http://_____
User Name: _____ Email: _____
Password: _____ Phone: _____
                                   Acct. #: _____
Email Log In: _____
Security Questions: _____
_____

Reminders: _____
_____

Site Name: _____ http://_____
User Name: _____ Email: _____
Password: _____ Phone: _____
                                   Acct. #: _____
Email Log In: _____
Security Questions: _____
_____

Reminders: _____
_____

Site Name: _____ http://_____
User Name: _____ Email: _____
Password: _____ Phone: _____
                                   Acct. #: _____
Email Log In: _____
Security Questions: _____
_____

Reminders: _____
_____

Site Name: _____ http://_____
User Name: _____ Email: _____
Password: _____ Phone: _____
                                   Acct. #: _____
Email Log In: _____
Security Questions: _____
_____

Reminders: _____
_____

Gg

Site Name: _____ http://_____
User Name: _____ Email: _____
Password: _____ Phone: _____
                                     Acct. #: _____
Email Log In: _____
Security Questions: _____
_____
Reminders: _____
_____

Site Name: _____ http://_____
User Name: _____ Email: _____
Password: _____ Phone: _____
                                     Acct. #: _____
Email Log In: _____
Security Questions: _____
_____
Reminders: _____
_____

Site Name: _____ http://_____
User Name: _____ Email: _____
Password: _____ Phone: _____
                                     Acct. #: _____
Email Log In: _____
Security Questions: _____
_____
Reminders: _____
_____

Site Name: _____ http://_____
User Name: _____ Email: _____
Password: _____ Phone: _____
                                     Acct. #: _____
Email Log In: _____
Security Questions: _____
_____
Reminders: _____
_____

Site Name: _____ http://_____
User Name: _____ Email: _____
Password: _____ Phone: _____
                                     Acct. #: _____
Email Log In: _____
Security Questions: _____
_____
Reminders: _____
_____

Gg

Site Name: _____ http://_____
User Name: _____ Email: _____
Password: _____ Phone: _____
                                      Acct. #: _____
Email Log In: _____
Security Questions: _____
_____
Reminders: _____
_____

Site Name: _____ http://_____
User Name: _____ Email: _____
Password: _____ Phone: _____
                                      Acct. #: _____
Email Log In: _____
Security Questions: _____
_____
Reminders: _____
_____

Site Name: _____ http://_____
User Name: _____ Email: _____
Password: _____ Phone: _____
                                      Acct. #: _____
Email Log In: _____
Security Questions: _____
_____
Reminders: _____
_____

Site Name: _____ http://_____
User Name: _____ Email: _____
Password: _____ Phone: _____
                                      Acct. #: _____
Email Log In: _____
Security Questions: _____
_____
Reminders: _____
_____

Site Name: _____ http://_____
User Name: _____ Email: _____
Password: _____ Phone: _____
                                      Acct. #: _____
Email Log In: _____
Security Questions: _____
_____
Reminders: _____
_____

Gg

Site Name: _____ http://_____
User Name: _____ Email: _____
Password: _____ Phone: _____
                                   Acct. #: _____
Email Log In: _____
Security Questions: _____
_____

Reminders: _____
_____

Site Name: _____ http://_____
User Name: _____ Email: _____
Password: _____ Phone: _____
                                   Acct. #: _____
Email Log In: _____
Security Questions: _____
_____

Reminders: _____
_____

Site Name: _____ http://_____
User Name: _____ Email: _____
Password: _____ Phone: _____
                                   Acct. #: _____
Email Log In: _____
Security Questions: _____
_____

Reminders: _____
_____

Site Name: _____ http://_____
User Name: _____ Email: _____
Password: _____ Phone: _____
                                   Acct. #: _____
Email Log In: _____
Security Questions: _____
_____

Reminders: _____
_____

Site Name: _____ http://_____
User Name: _____ Email: _____
Password: _____ Phone: _____
                                   Acct. #: _____
Email Log In: _____
Security Questions: _____
_____

Reminders: _____
_____

Gg

Site Name: _____ http://_____
User Name: _____ Email: _____
Password: _____ Phone: _____
                                   Acct. #: _____
Email Log In: _____
Security Questions: _____
_____
Reminders: _____
_____

Site Name: _____ http://_____
User Name: _____ Email: _____
Password: _____ Phone: _____
                                   Acct. #: _____
Email Log In: _____
Security Questions: _____
_____
Reminders: _____
_____

Site Name: _____ http://_____
User Name: _____ Email: _____
Password: _____ Phone: _____
                                   Acct. #: _____
Email Log In: _____
Security Questions: _____
_____
Reminders: _____
_____

Site Name: _____ http://_____
User Name: _____ Email: _____
Password: _____ Phone: _____
                                   Acct. #: _____
Email Log In: _____
Security Questions: _____
_____
Reminders: _____
_____

Site Name: _____ http://_____
User Name: _____ Email: _____
Password: _____ Phone: _____
                                   Acct. #: _____
Email Log In: _____
Security Questions: _____
_____
Reminders: _____
_____

Hh

Site Name: _____ http://_____
User Name: _____ Email: _____
Password: _____ Phone: _____
                                     Acct. #: _____
Email Log In: _____
Security Questions: _____
_____

Reminders: _____
_____

Site Name: _____ http://_____
User Name: _____ Email: _____
Password: _____ Phone: _____
                                     Acct. #: _____
Email Log In: _____
Security Questions: _____
_____

Reminders: _____
_____

Site Name: _____ http://_____
User Name: _____ Email: _____
Password: _____ Phone: _____
                                     Acct. #: _____
Email Log In: _____
Security Questions: _____
_____

Reminders: _____
_____

Site Name: _____ http://_____
User Name: _____ Email: _____
Password: _____ Phone: _____
                                     Acct. #: _____
Email Log In: _____
Security Questions: _____
_____

Reminders: _____
_____

Site Name: _____ http://_____
User Name: _____ Email: _____
Password: _____ Phone: _____
                                     Acct. #: _____
Email Log In: _____
Security Questions: _____
_____

Reminders: _____
_____

Hh

Site Name: _____ http://_____
User Name: _____ Email: _____
Password: _____ Phone: _____
                                      Acct. #: _____
Email Log In: _____
Security Questions: _____
_____
Reminders: _____
_____

Site Name: _____ http://_____
User Name: _____ Email: _____
Password: _____ Phone: _____
                                      Acct. #: _____
Email Log In: _____
Security Questions: _____
_____
Reminders: _____
_____

Site Name: _____ http://_____
User Name: _____ Email: _____
Password: _____ Phone: _____
                                      Acct. #: _____
Email Log In: _____
Security Questions: _____
_____
Reminders: _____
_____

Site Name: _____ http://_____
User Name: _____ Email: _____
Password: _____ Phone: _____
                                      Acct. #: _____
Email Log In: _____
Security Questions: _____
_____
Reminders: _____
_____

Site Name: _____ http://_____
User Name: _____ Email: _____
Password: _____ Phone: _____
                                      Acct. #: _____
Email Log In: _____
Security Questions: _____
_____
Reminders: _____
_____

Hh

Site Name: _____ http://_____
User Name: _____ Email: _____
Password: _____ Phone: _____
Acct. #: _____
Email Log In: _____
Security Questions: _____
_____
Reminders: _____
_____

Site Name: _____ http://_____
User Name: _____ Email: _____
Password: _____ Phone: _____
Acct. #: _____
Email Log In: _____
Security Questions: _____
_____
Reminders: _____
_____

Site Name: _____ http://_____
User Name: _____ Email: _____
Password: _____ Phone: _____
Acct. #: _____
Email Log In: _____
Security Questions: _____
_____
Reminders: _____
_____

Site Name: _____ http://_____
User Name: _____ Email: _____
Password: _____ Phone: _____
Acct. #: _____
Email Log In: _____
Security Questions: _____
_____
Reminders: _____
_____

Site Name: _____ http://_____
User Name: _____ Email: _____
Password: _____ Phone: _____
Acct. #: _____
Email Log In: _____
Security Questions: _____
_____
Reminders: _____
_____

Hh

Site Name: _____ http://_____

User Name: _____ Email: _____

Password: _____ Phone: _____

Acct. #: _____

Email Log In: _____

Security Questions: _____

_____

Reminders: _____

_____

Site Name: _____ http://_____

User Name: _____ Email: _____

Password: _____ Phone: _____

Acct. #: _____

Email Log In: _____

Security Questions: _____

_____

Reminders: _____

_____

Site Name: _____ http://_____

User Name: _____ Email: _____

Password: _____ Phone: _____

Acct. #: _____

Email Log In: _____

Security Questions: _____

_____

Reminders: _____

_____

Site Name: _____ http://_____

User Name: _____ Email: _____

Password: _____ Phone: _____

Acct. #: _____

Email Log In: _____

Security Questions: _____

_____

Reminders: _____

_____

Site Name: _____ http://_____

User Name: _____ Email: _____

Password: _____ Phone: _____

Acct. #: _____

Email Log In: _____

Security Questions: _____

_____

Reminders: _____

_____

Ii

Site Name: _____ http://_____
User Name: _____ Email: _____
Password: _____ Phone: _____
                                     Acct. #: _____
Email Log In: _____
Security Questions: _____
_____
Reminders: _____
_____

Site Name: _____ http://_____
User Name: _____ Email: _____
Password: _____ Phone: _____
                                     Acct. #: _____
Email Log In: _____
Security Questions: _____
_____
Reminders: _____
_____

Site Name: _____ http://_____
User Name: _____ Email: _____
Password: _____ Phone: _____
                                     Acct. #: _____
Email Log In: _____
Security Questions: _____
_____
Reminders: _____
_____

Site Name: _____ http://_____
User Name: _____ Email: _____
Password: _____ Phone: _____
                                     Acct. #: _____
Email Log In: _____
Security Questions: _____
_____
Reminders: _____
_____

Site Name: _____ http://_____
User Name: _____ Email: _____
Password: _____ Phone: _____
                                     Acct. #: _____
Email Log In: _____
Security Questions: _____
_____
Reminders: _____
_____

Ii

Site Name: _____ http://_____
User Name: _____ Email: _____
Password: _____ Phone: _____
Acct. #: _____

Email Log In: _____
Security Questions: _____
_____

Reminders: _____
_____

Site Name: _____ http://_____
User Name: _____ Email: _____
Password: _____ Phone: _____
Acct. #: _____

Email Log In: _____
Security Questions: _____
_____

Reminders: _____
_____

Site Name: _____ http://_____
User Name: _____ Email: _____
Password: _____ Phone: _____
Acct. #: _____

Email Log In: _____
Security Questions: _____
_____

Reminders: _____
_____

Site Name: _____ http://_____
User Name: _____ Email: _____
Password: _____ Phone: _____
Acct. #: _____

Email Log In: _____
Security Questions: _____
_____

Reminders: _____
_____

Site Name: _____ http://_____
User Name: _____ Email: _____
Password: _____ Phone: _____
Acct. #: _____

Email Log In: _____
Security Questions: _____
_____

Reminders: _____
_____

Ii

Site Name: _____ http://_____
User Name: _____ Email: _____
Password: _____ Phone: _____
Acct. #: _____
Email Log In: _____
Security Questions: _____
_____
Reminders: _____
_____

Site Name: _____ http://_____
User Name: _____ Email: _____
Password: _____ Phone: _____
Acct. #: _____
Email Log In: _____
Security Questions: _____
_____
Reminders: _____
_____

Site Name: _____ http://_____
User Name: _____ Email: _____
Password: _____ Phone: _____
Acct. #: _____
Email Log In: _____
Security Questions: _____
_____
Reminders: _____
_____

Site Name: _____ http://_____
User Name: _____ Email: _____
Password: _____ Phone: _____
Acct. #: _____
Email Log In: _____
Security Questions: _____
_____
Reminders: _____
_____

Site Name: _____ http://_____
User Name: _____ Email: _____
Password: _____ Phone: _____
Acct. #: _____
Email Log In: _____
Security Questions: _____
_____
Reminders: _____
_____

Ii

Site Name: _____ http://_____
User Name: _____ Email: _____
Password: _____ Phone: _____
_____ Acct. #: _____

Email Log In: _____
Security Questions: _____
_____

Reminders: _____
_____

Site Name: _____ http://_____
User Name: _____ Email: _____
Password: _____ Phone: _____
_____ Acct. #: _____

Email Log In: _____
Security Questions: _____
_____

Reminders: _____
_____

Site Name: _____ http://_____
User Name: _____ Email: _____
Password: _____ Phone: _____
_____ Acct. #: _____

Email Log In: _____
Security Questions: _____
_____

Reminders: _____
_____

Site Name: _____ http://_____
User Name: _____ Email: _____
Password: _____ Phone: _____
_____ Acct. #: _____

Email Log In: _____
Security Questions: _____
_____

Reminders: _____
_____

Site Name: _____ http://_____
User Name: _____ Email: _____
Password: _____ Phone: _____
_____ Acct. #: _____

Email Log In: _____
Security Questions: _____
_____

Reminders: _____
_____

Jj

Site Name: _____ http://_____
User Name: _____ Email: _____
Password: _____ Phone: _____
Acct. #: _____

Email Log In: _____
Security Questions: _____
_____

Reminders: _____
_____

Site Name: _____ http://_____
User Name: _____ Email: _____
Password: _____ Phone: _____
Acct. #: _____

Email Log In: _____
Security Questions: _____
_____

Reminders: _____
_____

Site Name: _____ http://_____
User Name: _____ Email: _____
Password: _____ Phone: _____
Acct. #: _____

Email Log In: _____
Security Questions: _____
_____

Reminders: _____
_____

Site Name: _____ http://_____
User Name: _____ Email: _____
Password: _____ Phone: _____
Acct. #: _____

Email Log In: _____
Security Questions: _____
_____

Reminders: _____
_____

Site Name: _____ http://_____
User Name: _____ Email: _____
Password: _____ Phone: _____
Acct. #: _____

Email Log In: _____
Security Questions: _____
_____

Reminders: _____
_____

Jj

Site Name: _____ http://_____
User Name: _____ Email: _____
Password: _____ Phone: _____
                                   Acct. #: _____
Email Log In: _____
Security Questions: _____
_____
Reminders: _____
_____

Site Name: _____ http://_____
User Name: _____ Email: _____
Password: _____ Phone: _____
                                   Acct. #: _____
Email Log In: _____
Security Questions: _____
_____
Reminders: _____
_____

Site Name: _____ http://_____
User Name: _____ Email: _____
Password: _____ Phone: _____
                                   Acct. #: _____
Email Log In: _____
Security Questions: _____
_____
Reminders: _____
_____

Site Name: _____ http://_____
User Name: _____ Email: _____
Password: _____ Phone: _____
                                   Acct. #: _____
Email Log In: _____
Security Questions: _____
_____
Reminders: _____
_____

Site Name: _____ http://_____
User Name: _____ Email: _____
Password: _____ Phone: _____
                                   Acct. #: _____
Email Log In: _____
Security Questions: _____
_____
Reminders: _____
_____

Jj

Site Name: _____ http://_____
User Name: _____ Email: _____
Password: _____ Phone: _____
                                     Acct. #: _____
Email Log In: _____
Security Questions: _____
_____
Reminders: _____
_____

Site Name: _____ http://_____
User Name: _____ Email: _____
Password: _____ Phone: _____
                                     Acct. #: _____
Email Log In: _____
Security Questions: _____
_____
Reminders: _____
_____

Site Name: _____ http://_____
User Name: _____ Email: _____
Password: _____ Phone: _____
                                     Acct. #: _____
Email Log In: _____
Security Questions: _____
_____
Reminders: _____
_____

Site Name: _____ http://_____
User Name: _____ Email: _____
Password: _____ Phone: _____
                                     Acct. #: _____
Email Log In: _____
Security Questions: _____
_____
Reminders: _____
_____

Site Name: _____ http://_____
User Name: _____ Email: _____
Password: _____ Phone: _____
                                     Acct. #: _____
Email Log In: _____
Security Questions: _____
_____
Reminders: _____
_____

Jj

Site Name: _____ http:// _____
User Name: _____ Email: _____
Password: _____ Phone: _____
                                      Acct. #: _____
Email Log In: _____
Security Questions: _____
_____
Reminders: _____
_____

Site Name: _____ http:// _____
User Name: _____ Email: _____
Password: _____ Phone: _____
                                      Acct. #: _____
Email Log In: _____
Security Questions: _____
_____
Reminders: _____
_____

Site Name: _____ http:// _____
User Name: _____ Email: _____
Password: _____ Phone: _____
                                      Acct. #: _____
Email Log In: _____
Security Questions: _____
_____
Reminders: _____
_____

Site Name: _____ http:// _____
User Name: _____ Email: _____
Password: _____ Phone: _____
                                      Acct. #: _____
Email Log In: _____
Security Questions: _____
_____
Reminders: _____
_____

Site Name: _____ http:// _____
User Name: _____ Email: _____
Password: _____ Phone: _____
                                      Acct. #: _____
Email Log In: _____
Security Questions: _____
_____
Reminders: _____
_____

Kk

Site Name: _____ http://_____
User Name: _____ Email: _____
Password: _____ Phone: _____
Acct. #: _____
Email Log In: _____
Security Questions: _____
_____
Reminders: _____
_____

Site Name: _____ http://_____
User Name: _____ Email: _____
Password: _____ Phone: _____
Acct. #: _____
Email Log In: _____
Security Questions: _____
_____
Reminders: _____
_____

Site Name: _____ http://_____
User Name: _____ Email: _____
Password: _____ Phone: _____
Acct. #: _____
Email Log In: _____
Security Questions: _____
_____
Reminders: _____
_____

Site Name: _____ http://_____
User Name: _____ Email: _____
Password: _____ Phone: _____
Acct. #: _____
Email Log In: _____
Security Questions: _____
_____
Reminders: _____
_____

Site Name: _____ http://_____
User Name: _____ Email: _____
Password: _____ Phone: _____
Acct. #: _____
Email Log In: _____
Security Questions: _____
_____
Reminders: _____
_____

Kk

Site Name: _____ http://_____
User Name: _____ Email: _____
Password: _____ Phone: _____
                                      Acct. #: _____
Email Log In: _____
Security Questions: _____
_____

Reminders: _____
_____

Site Name: _____ http://_____
User Name: _____ Email: _____
Password: _____ Phone: _____
                                      Acct. #: _____
Email Log In: _____
Security Questions: _____
_____

Reminders: _____
_____

Site Name: _____ http://_____
User Name: _____ Email: _____
Password: _____ Phone: _____
                                      Acct. #: _____
Email Log In: _____
Security Questions: _____
_____

Reminders: _____
_____

Site Name: _____ http://_____
User Name: _____ Email: _____
Password: _____ Phone: _____
                                      Acct. #: _____
Email Log In: _____
Security Questions: _____
_____

Reminders: _____
_____

Site Name: _____ http://_____
User Name: _____ Email: _____
Password: _____ Phone: _____
                                      Acct. #: _____
Email Log In: _____
Security Questions: _____
_____

Reminders: _____
_____

Kk

Site Name: _____ http://_____
User Name: _____ Email: _____
Password: _____ Phone: _____
                                      Acct. #: _____
Email Log In: _____
Security Questions: _____
_____

Reminders: _____
_____

Site Name: _____ http://_____
User Name: _____ Email: _____
Password: _____ Phone: _____
                                      Acct. #: _____
Email Log In: _____
Security Questions: _____
_____

Reminders: _____
_____

Site Name: _____ http://_____
User Name: _____ Email: _____
Password: _____ Phone: _____
                                      Acct. #: _____
Email Log In: _____
Security Questions: _____
_____

Reminders: _____
_____

Site Name: _____ http://_____
User Name: _____ Email: _____
Password: _____ Phone: _____
                                      Acct. #: _____
Email Log In: _____
Security Questions: _____
_____

Reminders: _____
_____

Site Name: _____ http://_____
User Name: _____ Email: _____
Password: _____ Phone: _____
                                      Acct. #: _____
Email Log In: _____
Security Questions: _____
_____

Reminders: _____
_____

Kk

Site Name: _____ http://_____
User Name: _____ Email: _____
Password: _____ Phone: _____
                                       Acct. #: _____
Email Log In: _____
Security Questions: _____
_____
Reminders: _____
_____

Site Name: _____ http://_____
User Name: _____ Email: _____
Password: _____ Phone: _____
                                       Acct. #: _____
Email Log In: _____
Security Questions: _____
_____
Reminders: _____
_____

Site Name: _____ http://_____
User Name: _____ Email: _____
Password: _____ Phone: _____
                                       Acct. #: _____
Email Log In: _____
Security Questions: _____
_____
Reminders: _____
_____

Site Name: _____ http://_____
User Name: _____ Email: _____
Password: _____ Phone: _____
                                       Acct. #: _____
Email Log In: _____
Security Questions: _____
_____
Reminders: _____
_____

Site Name: _____ http://_____
User Name: _____ Email: _____
Password: _____ Phone: _____
                                       Acct. #: _____
Email Log In: _____
Security Questions: _____
_____
Reminders: _____
_____

Site Name: _____ http:// _____
User Name: _____ Email: _____
Password: _____ Phone: _____
Acct. #: _____
Email Log In: _____
Security Questions: _____
_____
Reminders: _____
_____

Site Name: _____ http:// _____
User Name: _____ Email: _____
Password: _____ Phone: _____
Acct. #: _____
Email Log In: _____
Security Questions: _____
_____
Reminders: _____
_____

Site Name: _____ http:// _____
User Name: _____ Email: _____
Password: _____ Phone: _____
Acct. #: _____
Email Log In: _____
Security Questions: _____
_____
Reminders: _____
_____

Site Name: _____ http:// _____
User Name: _____ Email: _____
Password: _____ Phone: _____
Acct. #: _____
Email Log In: _____
Security Questions: _____
_____
Reminders: _____
_____

Site Name: _____ http:// _____
User Name: _____ Email: _____
Password: _____ Phone: _____
Acct. #: _____
Email Log In: _____
Security Questions: _____
_____
Reminders: _____
_____

L1

Site Name: _____ http://_____
User Name: _____ Email: _____
Password: _____ Phone: _____
                                     Acct. #: _____
Email Log In: _____
Security Questions: _____
_____
Reminders: _____
_____

Site Name: _____ http://_____
User Name: _____ Email: _____
Password: _____ Phone: _____
                                     Acct. #: _____
Email Log In: _____
Security Questions: _____
_____
Reminders: _____
_____

Site Name: _____ http://_____
User Name: _____ Email: _____
Password: _____ Phone: _____
                                     Acct. #: _____
Email Log In: _____
Security Questions: _____
_____
Reminders: _____
_____

Site Name: _____ http://_____
User Name: _____ Email: _____
Password: _____ Phone: _____
                                     Acct. #: _____
Email Log In: _____
Security Questions: _____
_____
Reminders: _____
_____

Site Name: _____ http://_____
User Name: _____ Email: _____
Password: _____ Phone: _____
                                     Acct. #: _____
Email Log In: _____
Security Questions: _____
_____
Reminders: _____
_____

L1

Site Name: _____ http://_____
User Name: _____ Email: _____
Password: _____ Phone: _____
                                      Acct. #: _____
Email Log In: _____
Security Questions: _____
_____
Reminders: _____
_____

Site Name: _____ http://_____
User Name: _____ Email: _____
Password: _____ Phone: _____
                                      Acct. #: _____
Email Log In: _____
Security Questions: _____
_____
Reminders: _____
_____

Site Name: _____ http://_____
User Name: _____ Email: _____
Password: _____ Phone: _____
                                      Acct. #: _____
Email Log In: _____
Security Questions: _____
_____
Reminders: _____
_____

Site Name: _____ http://_____
User Name: _____ Email: _____
Password: _____ Phone: _____
                                      Acct. #: _____
Email Log In: _____
Security Questions: _____
_____
Reminders: _____
_____

Site Name: _____ http://_____
User Name: _____ Email: _____
Password: _____ Phone: _____
                                      Acct. #: _____
Email Log In: _____
Security Questions: _____
_____
Reminders: _____
_____

L1

Site Name: _____ http://_____
User Name: _____ Email: _____
Password: _____ Phone: _____
                                                   Acct. #: _____
Email Log In: _____
Security Questions: _____
_____
Reminders: _____
_____

Site Name: _____ http://_____
User Name: _____ Email: _____
Password: _____ Phone: _____
                                                   Acct. #: _____
Email Log In: _____
Security Questions: _____
_____
Reminders: _____
_____

Site Name: _____ http://_____
User Name: _____ Email: _____
Password: _____ Phone: _____
                                                   Acct. #: _____
Email Log In: _____
Security Questions: _____
_____
Reminders: _____
_____

Site Name: _____ http://_____
User Name: _____ Email: _____
Password: _____ Phone: _____
                                                   Acct. #: _____
Email Log In: _____
Security Questions: _____
_____
Reminders: _____
_____

Site Name: _____ http://_____
User Name: _____ Email: _____
Password: _____ Phone: _____
                                                   Acct. #: _____
Email Log In: _____
Security Questions: _____
_____
Reminders: _____
_____

Mm

Site Name: _____ http://_____
User Name: _____ Email: _____
Password: _____ Phone: _____
Acct. #: _____

Email Log In: _____
Security Questions: _____
_____

Reminders: _____
_____

Site Name: _____ http://_____
User Name: _____ Email: _____
Password: _____ Phone: _____
Acct. #: _____

Email Log In: _____
Security Questions: _____
_____

Reminders: _____
_____

Site Name: _____ http://_____
User Name: _____ Email: _____
Password: _____ Phone: _____
Acct. #: _____

Email Log In: _____
Security Questions: _____
_____

Reminders: _____
_____

Site Name: _____ http://_____
User Name: _____ Email: _____
Password: _____ Phone: _____
Acct. #: _____

Email Log In: _____
Security Questions: _____
_____

Reminders: _____
_____

Site Name: _____ http://_____
User Name: _____ Email: _____
Password: _____ Phone: _____
Acct. #: _____

Email Log In: _____
Security Questions: _____
_____

Reminders: _____
_____

Mm

Site Name: _____ http://_____
User Name: _____ Email: _____
Password: _____ Phone: _____
                                     Acct. #: _____
Email Log In: _____
Security Questions: _____
_____
Reminders: _____
_____

Site Name: _____ http://_____
User Name: _____ Email: _____
Password: _____ Phone: _____
                                     Acct. #: _____
Email Log In: _____
Security Questions: _____
_____
Reminders: _____
_____

Site Name: _____ http://_____
User Name: _____ Email: _____
Password: _____ Phone: _____
                                     Acct. #: _____
Email Log In: _____
Security Questions: _____
_____
Reminders: _____
_____

Site Name: _____ http://_____
User Name: _____ Email: _____
Password: _____ Phone: _____
                                     Acct. #: _____
Email Log In: _____
Security Questions: _____
_____
Reminders: _____
_____

Site Name: _____ http://_____
User Name: _____ Email: _____
Password: _____ Phone: _____
                                     Acct. #: _____
Email Log In: _____
Security Questions: _____
_____
Reminders: _____
_____

Mm

Site Name: _____ http://_____
User Name: _____ Email: _____
Password: _____ Phone: _____
                                                   Acct. #: _____
Email Log In: _____
Security Questions: _____
_____
Reminders: _____
_____

Site Name: _____ http://_____
User Name: _____ Email: _____
Password: _____ Phone: _____
                                                   Acct. #: _____
Email Log In: _____
Security Questions: _____
_____
Reminders: _____
_____

Site Name: _____ http://_____
User Name: _____ Email: _____
Password: _____ Phone: _____
                                                   Acct. #: _____
Email Log In: _____
Security Questions: _____
_____
Reminders: _____
_____

Site Name: _____ http://_____
User Name: _____ Email: _____
Password: _____ Phone: _____
                                                   Acct. #: _____
Email Log In: _____
Security Questions: _____
_____
Reminders: _____
_____

Site Name: _____ http://_____
User Name: _____ Email: _____
Password: _____ Phone: _____
                                                   Acct. #: _____
Email Log In: _____
Security Questions: _____
_____
Reminders: _____
_____

Mm

Site Name: _____ http://_____
User Name: _____ Email: _____
Password: _____ Phone: _____
                                     Acct. #: _____
Email Log In: _____
Security Questions: _____
_____
Reminders: _____
_____

Site Name: _____ http://_____
User Name: _____ Email: _____
Password: _____ Phone: _____
                                     Acct. #: _____
Email Log In: _____
Security Questions: _____
_____
Reminders: _____
_____

Site Name: _____ http://_____
User Name: _____ Email: _____
Password: _____ Phone: _____
                                     Acct. #: _____
Email Log In: _____
Security Questions: _____
_____
Reminders: _____
_____

Site Name: _____ http://_____
User Name: _____ Email: _____
Password: _____ Phone: _____
                                     Acct. #: _____
Email Log In: _____
Security Questions: _____
_____
Reminders: _____
_____

Site Name: _____ http://_____
User Name: _____ Email: _____
Password: _____ Phone: _____
                                     Acct. #: _____
Email Log In: _____
Security Questions: _____
_____
Reminders: _____
_____

Nn

Site Name: _____ http://_____
User Name: _____ Email: _____
Password: _____ Phone: _____
                                                        Acct. #: _____
Email Log In: _____
Security Questions: _____
_____
Reminders: _____
_____

Site Name: _____ http://_____
User Name: _____ Email: _____
Password: _____ Phone: _____
                                                        Acct. #: _____
Email Log In: _____
Security Questions: _____
_____
Reminders: _____
_____

Site Name: _____ http://_____
User Name: _____ Email: _____
Password: _____ Phone: _____
                                                        Acct. #: _____
Email Log In: _____
Security Questions: _____
_____
Reminders: _____
_____

Site Name: _____ http://_____
User Name: _____ Email: _____
Password: _____ Phone: _____
                                                        Acct. #: _____
Email Log In: _____
Security Questions: _____
_____
Reminders: _____
_____

Site Name: _____ http://_____
User Name: _____ Email: _____
Password: _____ Phone: _____
                                                        Acct. #: _____
Email Log In: _____
Security Questions: _____
_____
Reminders: _____
_____

Nn

Site Name: _____ http://_____

User Name: _____ Email: _____

Password: _____ Phone: _____

Acct. #: _____

Email Log In: _____

Security Questions: _____

_____

Reminders: _____

_____

Site Name: _____ http://_____

User Name: _____ Email: _____

Password: _____ Phone: _____

Acct. #: _____

Email Log In: _____

Security Questions: _____

_____

Reminders: _____

_____

Site Name: _____ http://_____

User Name: _____ Email: _____

Password: _____ Phone: _____

Acct. #: _____

Email Log In: _____

Security Questions: _____

_____

Reminders: _____

_____

Site Name: _____ http://_____

User Name: _____ Email: _____

Password: _____ Phone: _____

Acct. #: _____

Email Log In: _____

Security Questions: _____

_____

Reminders: _____

_____

Site Name: _____ http://_____

User Name: _____ Email: _____

Password: _____ Phone: _____

Acct. #: _____

Email Log In: _____

Security Questions: _____

_____

Reminders: _____

_____

Nn

Site Name: _____ http://_____
User Name: _____ Email: _____
Password: _____ Phone: _____
Acct. #: _____
Email Log In: _____
Security Questions: _____
_____

Reminders: _____
_____

Site Name: _____ http://_____
User Name: _____ Email: _____
Password: _____ Phone: _____
Acct. #: _____
Email Log In: _____
Security Questions: _____
_____

Reminders: _____
_____

Site Name: _____ http://_____
User Name: _____ Email: _____
Password: _____ Phone: _____
Acct. #: _____
Email Log In: _____
Security Questions: _____
_____

Reminders: _____
_____

Site Name: _____ http://_____
User Name: _____ Email: _____
Password: _____ Phone: _____
Acct. #: _____
Email Log In: _____
Security Questions: _____
_____

Reminders: _____
_____

Site Name: _____ http://_____
User Name: _____ Email: _____
Password: _____ Phone: _____
Acct. #: _____
Email Log In: _____
Security Questions: _____
_____

Reminders: _____
_____

Nn

Site Name: _____ http://_____
User Name: _____ Email: _____
Password: _____ Phone: _____
                                   Acct. #: _____
Email Log In: _____
Security Questions: _____
_____
Reminders: _____
_____

Site Name: _____ http://_____
User Name: _____ Email: _____
Password: _____ Phone: _____
                                   Acct. #: _____
Email Log In: _____
Security Questions: _____
_____
Reminders: _____
_____

Site Name: _____ http://_____
User Name: _____ Email: _____
Password: _____ Phone: _____
                                   Acct. #: _____
Email Log In: _____
Security Questions: _____
_____
Reminders: _____
_____

Site Name: _____ http://_____
User Name: _____ Email: _____
Password: _____ Phone: _____
                                   Acct. #: _____
Email Log In: _____
Security Questions: _____
_____
Reminders: _____
_____

Site Name: _____ http://_____
User Name: _____ Email: _____
Password: _____ Phone: _____
                                   Acct. #: _____
Email Log In: _____
Security Questions: _____
_____
Reminders: _____
_____

Site Name: _____ http://_____
User Name: _____ Email: _____
Password: _____ Phone: _____
                                     Acct. #: _____
Email Log In: _____
Security Questions: _____
_____

Reminders: _____
_____

Site Name: _____ http://_____
User Name: _____ Email: _____
Password: _____ Phone: _____
                                     Acct. #: _____
Email Log In: _____
Security Questions: _____
_____

Reminders: _____
_____

Site Name: _____ http://_____
User Name: _____ Email: _____
Password: _____ Phone: _____
                                     Acct. #: _____
Email Log In: _____
Security Questions: _____
_____

Reminders: _____
_____

Site Name: _____ http://_____
User Name: _____ Email: _____
Password: _____ Phone: _____
                                     Acct. #: _____
Email Log In: _____
Security Questions: _____
_____

Reminders: _____
_____

Site Name: _____ http://_____
User Name: _____ Email: _____
Password: _____ Phone: _____
                                     Acct. #: _____
Email Log In: _____
Security Questions: _____
_____

Reminders: _____
_____

Oo

Site Name: _____ http://_____
User Name: _____ Email: _____
Password: _____ Phone: _____
                                      Acct. #: _____
Email Log In: _____
Security Questions: _____
_____
Reminders: _____
_____

Site Name: _____ http://_____
User Name: _____ Email: _____
Password: _____ Phone: _____
                                      Acct. #: _____
Email Log In: _____
Security Questions: _____
_____
Reminders: _____
_____

Site Name: _____ http://_____
User Name: _____ Email: _____
Password: _____ Phone: _____
                                      Acct. #: _____
Email Log In: _____
Security Questions: _____
_____
Reminders: _____
_____

Site Name: _____ http://_____
User Name: _____ Email: _____
Password: _____ Phone: _____
                                      Acct. #: _____
Email Log In: _____
Security Questions: _____
_____
Reminders: _____
_____

Site Name: _____ http://_____
User Name: _____ Email: _____
Password: _____ Phone: _____
                                      Acct. #: _____
Email Log In: _____
Security Questions: _____
_____
Reminders: _____
_____

Site Name: _____ http://_____
User Name: _____ Email: _____
Password: _____ Phone: _____
Acct. #: _____
Email Log In: _____
Security Questions: _____
_____

Reminders: _____
_____

Site Name: _____ http://_____
User Name: _____ Email: _____
Password: _____ Phone: _____
Acct. #: _____
Email Log In: _____
Security Questions: _____
_____

Reminders: _____
_____

Site Name: _____ http://_____
User Name: _____ Email: _____
Password: _____ Phone: _____
Acct. #: _____
Email Log In: _____
Security Questions: _____
_____

Reminders: _____
_____

Site Name: _____ http://_____
User Name: _____ Email: _____
Password: _____ Phone: _____
Acct. #: _____
Email Log In: _____
Security Questions: _____
_____

Reminders: _____
_____

Site Name: _____ http://_____
User Name: _____ Email: _____
Password: _____ Phone: _____
Acct. #: _____
Email Log In: _____
Security Questions: _____
_____

Reminders: _____
_____

Oo

Site Name: _____ http://_____
User Name: _____ Email: _____
Password: _____ Phone: _____
Acct. #: _____
Email Log In: _____
Security Questions: _____
_____
Reminders: _____
_____

Site Name: _____ http://_____
User Name: _____ Email: _____
Password: _____ Phone: _____
Acct. #: _____
Email Log In: _____
Security Questions: _____
_____
Reminders: _____
_____

Site Name: _____ http://_____
User Name: _____ Email: _____
Password: _____ Phone: _____
Acct. #: _____
Email Log In: _____
Security Questions: _____
_____
Reminders: _____
_____

Site Name: _____ http://_____
User Name: _____ Email: _____
Password: _____ Phone: _____
Acct. #: _____
Email Log In: _____
Security Questions: _____
_____
Reminders: _____
_____

Site Name: _____ http://_____
User Name: _____ Email: _____
Password: _____ Phone: _____
Acct. #: _____
Email Log In: _____
Security Questions: _____
_____
Reminders: _____
_____

Pp

Site Name: _____ http://_____
User Name: _____ Email: _____
Password: _____ Phone: _____
                                      Acct. #: _____
Email Log In: _____
Security Questions: _____
_____
Reminders: _____
_____

Site Name: _____ http://_____
User Name: _____ Email: _____
Password: _____ Phone: _____
                                      Acct. #: _____
Email Log In: _____
Security Questions: _____
_____
Reminders: _____
_____

Site Name: _____ http://_____
User Name: _____ Email: _____
Password: _____ Phone: _____
                                      Acct. #: _____
Email Log In: _____
Security Questions: _____
_____
Reminders: _____
_____

Site Name: _____ http://_____
User Name: _____ Email: _____
Password: _____ Phone: _____
                                      Acct. #: _____
Email Log In: _____
Security Questions: _____
_____
Reminders: _____
_____

Site Name: _____ http://_____
User Name: _____ Email: _____
Password: _____ Phone: _____
                                      Acct. #: _____
Email Log In: _____
Security Questions: _____
_____
Reminders: _____
_____

Pp

Site Name: _____ http:// _____
User Name: _____ Email: _____
Password: _____ Phone: _____
                                       Acct. #: _____
Email Log In: _____
Security Questions: _____
_____
Reminders: _____
_____

Site Name: _____ http:// _____
User Name: _____ Email: _____
Password: _____ Phone: _____
                                       Acct. #: _____
Email Log In: _____
Security Questions: _____
_____
Reminders: _____
_____

Site Name: _____ http:// _____
User Name: _____ Email: _____
Password: _____ Phone: _____
                                       Acct. #: _____
Email Log In: _____
Security Questions: _____
_____
Reminders: _____
_____

Site Name: _____ http:// _____
User Name: _____ Email: _____
Password: _____ Phone: _____
                                       Acct. #: _____
Email Log In: _____
Security Questions: _____
_____
Reminders: _____
_____

Site Name: _____ http:// _____
User Name: _____ Email: _____
Password: _____ Phone: _____
                                       Acct. #: _____
Email Log In: _____
Security Questions: _____
_____
Reminders: _____
_____

Pp

Site Name: _____ http://_____
User Name: _____ Email: _____
Password: _____ Phone: _____
                                       Acct. #: _____
Email Log In: _____
Security Questions: _____
_____
Reminders: _____
_____

Site Name: _____ http://_____
User Name: _____ Email: _____
Password: _____ Phone: _____
                                       Acct. #: _____
Email Log In: _____
Security Questions: _____
_____
Reminders: _____
_____

Site Name: _____ http://_____
User Name: _____ Email: _____
Password: _____ Phone: _____
                                       Acct. #: _____
Email Log In: _____
Security Questions: _____
_____
Reminders: _____
_____

Site Name: _____ http://_____
User Name: _____ Email: _____
Password: _____ Phone: _____
                                       Acct. #: _____
Email Log In: _____
Security Questions: _____
_____
Reminders: _____
_____

Site Name: _____ http://_____
User Name: _____ Email: _____
Password: _____ Phone: _____
                                       Acct. #: _____
Email Log In: _____
Security Questions: _____
_____
Reminders: _____
_____

Pp

Site Name: _____ http:// _____
User Name: _____ Email: _____
Password: _____ Phone: _____
                                   Acct. #: _____
Email Log In: _____
Security Questions: _____
_____

Reminders: _____
_____

Site Name: _____ http:// _____
User Name: _____ Email: _____
Password: _____ Phone: _____
                                   Acct. #: _____
Email Log In: _____
Security Questions: _____
_____

Reminders: _____
_____

Site Name: _____ http:// _____
User Name: _____ Email: _____
Password: _____ Phone: _____
                                   Acct. #: _____
Email Log In: _____
Security Questions: _____
_____

Reminders: _____
_____

Site Name: _____ http:// _____
User Name: _____ Email: _____
Password: _____ Phone: _____
                                   Acct. #: _____
Email Log In: _____
Security Questions: _____
_____

Reminders: _____
_____

Site Name: _____ http:// _____
User Name: _____ Email: _____
Password: _____ Phone: _____
                                   Acct. #: _____
Email Log In: _____
Security Questions: _____
_____

Reminders: _____
_____

Qq

Site Name: _____ http://_____
User Name: _____ Email: _____
Password: _____ Phone: _____
Acct. #: _____

Email Log In: _____
Security Questions: _____
_____

Reminders: _____
_____

Site Name: _____ http://_____
User Name: _____ Email: _____
Password: _____ Phone: _____
Acct. #: _____

Email Log In: _____
Security Questions: _____
_____

Reminders: _____
_____

Site Name: _____ http://_____
User Name: _____ Email: _____
Password: _____ Phone: _____
Acct. #: _____

Email Log In: _____
Security Questions: _____
_____

Reminders: _____
_____

Site Name: _____ http://_____
User Name: _____ Email: _____
Password: _____ Phone: _____
Acct. #: _____

Email Log In: _____
Security Questions: _____
_____

Reminders: _____
_____

Site Name: _____ http://_____
User Name: _____ Email: _____
Password: _____ Phone: _____
Acct. #: _____

Email Log In: _____
Security Questions: _____
_____

Reminders: _____
_____

Qq

Site Name: _____ http://_____
User Name: _____ Email: _____
Password: _____ Phone: _____
                                     Acct. #: _____
Email Log In: _____
Security Questions: _____
_____

Reminders: _____
_____

Site Name: _____ http://_____
User Name: _____ Email: _____
Password: _____ Phone: _____
                                     Acct. #: _____
Email Log In: _____
Security Questions: _____
_____

Reminders: _____
_____

Site Name: _____ http://_____
User Name: _____ Email: _____
Password: _____ Phone: _____
                                     Acct. #: _____
Email Log In: _____
Security Questions: _____
_____

Reminders: _____
_____

Site Name: _____ http://_____
User Name: _____ Email: _____
Password: _____ Phone: _____
                                     Acct. #: _____
Email Log In: _____
Security Questions: _____
_____

Reminders: _____
_____

Site Name: _____ http://_____
User Name: _____ Email: _____
Password: _____ Phone: _____
                                     Acct. #: _____
Email Log In: _____
Security Questions: _____
_____

Reminders: _____
_____

Rr

Site Name: _____ http://_____
User Name: _____ Email: _____
Password: _____ Phone: _____
                                               Acct. #: _____
Email Log In: _____
Security Questions: _____
_____
Reminders: _____
_____

Site Name: _____ http://_____
User Name: _____ Email: _____
Password: _____ Phone: _____
                                                 Acct. #: _____
Email Log In: _____
Security Questions: _____
_____
Reminders: _____
_____

Site Name: _____ http://_____
User Name: _____ Email: _____
Password: _____ Phone: _____
                                                 Acct. #: _____
Email Log In: _____
Security Questions: _____
_____
Reminders: _____
_____

Site Name: _____ http://_____
User Name: _____ Email: _____
Password: _____ Phone: _____
                                                 Acct. #: _____
Email Log In: _____
Security Questions: _____
_____
Reminders: _____
_____

Site Name: _____ http://_____
User Name: _____ Email: _____
Password: _____ Phone: _____
                                                 Acct. #: _____
Email Log In: _____
Security Questions: _____
_____
Reminders: _____
_____

Rr

Site Name: _____ http://_____
User Name: _____ Email: _____
Password: _____ Phone: _____
                                     Acct. #: _____
Email Log In: _____
Security Questions: _____
_____
Reminders: _____
_____

Site Name: _____ http://_____
User Name: _____ Email: _____
Password: _____ Phone: _____
                                     Acct. #: _____
Email Log In: _____
Security Questions: _____
_____
Reminders: _____
_____

Site Name: _____ http://_____
User Name: _____ Email: _____
Password: _____ Phone: _____
                                     Acct. #: _____
Email Log In: _____
Security Questions: _____
_____
Reminders: _____
_____

Site Name: _____ http://_____
User Name: _____ Email: _____
Password: _____ Phone: _____
                                     Acct. #: _____
Email Log In: _____
Security Questions: _____
_____
Reminders: _____
_____

Site Name: _____ http://_____
User Name: _____ Email: _____
Password: _____ Phone: _____
                                     Acct. #: _____
Email Log In: _____
Security Questions: _____
_____
Reminders: _____
_____

Rr

Site Name: _____ http://_____
User Name: _____ Email: _____
Password: _____ Phone: _____
                                      Acct. #: _____
Email Log In: _____
Security Questions: _____
_____

Reminders: _____
_____

Site Name: _____ http://_____
User Name: _____ Email: _____
Password: _____ Phone: _____
                                      Acct. #: _____
Email Log In: _____
Security Questions: _____
_____

Reminders: _____
_____

Site Name: _____ http://_____
User Name: _____ Email: _____
Password: _____ Phone: _____
                                      Acct. #: _____
Email Log In: _____
Security Questions: _____
_____

Reminders: _____
_____

Site Name: _____ http://_____
User Name: _____ Email: _____
Password: _____ Phone: _____
                                      Acct. #: _____
Email Log In: _____
Security Questions: _____
_____

Reminders: _____
_____

Site Name: _____ http://_____
User Name: _____ Email: _____
Password: _____ Phone: _____
                                      Acct. #: _____
Email Log In: _____
Security Questions: _____
_____

Reminders: _____
_____

Rr

Site Name: _____ http://_____
User Name: _____ Email: _____
Password: _____ Phone: _____
                                     Acct. #: _____
Email Log In: _____
Security Questions: _____
_____

Reminders: _____
_____

Site Name: _____ http://_____
User Name: _____ Email: _____
Password: _____ Phone: _____
                                     Acct. #: _____
Email Log In: _____
Security Questions: _____
_____

Reminders: _____
_____

Site Name: _____ http://_____
User Name: _____ Email: _____
Password: _____ Phone: _____
                                     Acct. #: _____
Email Log In: _____
Security Questions: _____
_____

Reminders: _____
_____

Site Name: _____ http://_____
User Name: _____ Email: _____
Password: _____ Phone: _____
                                     Acct. #: _____
Email Log In: _____
Security Questions: _____
_____

Reminders: _____
_____

Site Name: _____ http://_____
User Name: _____ Email: _____
Password: _____ Phone: _____
                                     Acct. #: _____
Email Log In: _____
Security Questions: _____
_____

Reminders: _____
_____

Ss

Site Name: _____ http://_____

User Name: _____ Email: _____

Password: _____ Phone: _____

Acct. #: _____

Email Log In: _____

Security Questions: _____

_____

Reminders: _____

_____

Site Name: _____ http://_____

User Name: _____ Email: _____

Password: _____ Phone: _____

Acct. #: _____

Email Log In: _____

Security Questions: _____

_____

Reminders: _____

_____

Site Name: _____ http://_____

User Name: _____ Email: _____

Password: _____ Phone: _____

Acct. #: _____

Email Log In: _____

Security Questions: _____

_____

Reminders: _____

_____

Site Name: _____ http://_____

User Name: _____ Email: _____

Password: _____ Phone: _____

Acct. #: _____

Email Log In: _____

Security Questions: _____

_____

Reminders: _____

_____

Site Name: _____ http://_____

User Name: _____ Email: _____

Password: _____ Phone: _____

Acct. #: _____

Email Log In: _____

Security Questions: _____

_____

Reminders: _____

_____

Ss

Site Name: _____ http://_____
User Name: _____ Email: _____
Password: _____ Phone: _____
                                     Acct. #: _____
Email Log In: _____
Security Questions: _____
_____
Reminders: _____
_____

Site Name: _____ http://_____
User Name: _____ Email: _____
Password: _____ Phone: _____
                                     Acct. #: _____
Email Log In: _____
Security Questions: _____
_____
Reminders: _____
_____

Site Name: _____ http://_____
User Name: _____ Email: _____
Password: _____ Phone: _____
                                     Acct. #: _____
Email Log In: _____
Security Questions: _____
_____
Reminders: _____
_____

Site Name: _____ http://_____
User Name: _____ Email: _____
Password: _____ Phone: _____
                                     Acct. #: _____
Email Log In: _____
Security Questions: _____
_____
Reminders: _____
_____

Site Name: _____ http://_____
User Name: _____ Email: _____
Password: _____ Phone: _____
                                     Acct. #: _____
Email Log In: _____
Security Questions: _____
_____
Reminders: _____
_____

Ss

Site Name: _____ http://_____
User Name: _____ Email: _____
Password: _____Phone: _____
Acct. #: _____
Email Log In: _____
Security Questions: _____
_____
Reminders: _____
_____

Site Name: _____ http://_____
User Name: _____ Email: _____
Password: _____Phone: _____
Acct. #: _____
Email Log In: _____
Security Questions: _____
_____
Reminders: _____
_____

Site Name: _____ http://_____
User Name: _____ Email: _____
Password: _____Phone: _____
Acct. #: _____
Email Log In: _____
Security Questions: _____
_____
Reminders: _____
_____

Site Name: _____ http://_____
User Name: _____ Email: _____
Password: _____Phone: _____
Acct. #: _____
Email Log In: _____
Security Questions: _____
_____
Reminders: _____
_____

Site Name: _____ http://_____
User Name: _____ Email: _____
Password: _____Phone: _____
Acct. #: _____
Email Log In: _____
Security Questions: _____
_____
Reminders: _____
_____

Ss

Site Name: _____ http://_____
User Name: _____ Email: _____
Password: _____ Phone: _____
                                      Acct. #: _____
Email Log In: _____
Security Questions: _____
_____
Reminders: _____
_____

Site Name: _____ http://_____
User Name: _____ Email: _____
Password: _____ Phone: _____
                                      Acct. #: _____
Email Log In: _____
Security Questions: _____
_____
Reminders: _____
_____

Site Name: _____ http://_____
User Name: _____ Email: _____
Password: _____ Phone: _____
                                      Acct. #: _____
Email Log In: _____
Security Questions: _____
_____
Reminders: _____
_____

Site Name: _____ http://_____
User Name: _____ Email: _____
Password: _____ Phone: _____
                                      Acct. #: _____
Email Log In: _____
Security Questions: _____
_____
Reminders: _____
_____

Site Name: _____ http://_____
User Name: _____ Email: _____
Password: _____ Phone: _____
                                      Acct. #: _____
Email Log In: _____
Security Questions: _____
_____
Reminders: _____
_____

Tt

Site Name: _____ http://_____
User Name: _____ Email: _____
Password: _____ Phone: _____
Acct. #: _____
Email Log In: _____
Security Questions: _____
_____
Reminders: _____
_____

Site Name: _____ http://_____
User Name: _____ Email: _____
Password: _____ Phone: _____
Acct. #: _____
Email Log In: _____
Security Questions: _____
_____
Reminders: _____
_____

Site Name: _____ http://_____
User Name: _____ Email: _____
Password: _____ Phone: _____
Acct. #: _____
Email Log In: _____
Security Questions: _____
_____
Reminders: _____
_____

Site Name: _____ http://_____
User Name: _____ Email: _____
Password: _____ Phone: _____
Acct. #: _____
Email Log In: _____
Security Questions: _____
_____
Reminders: _____
_____

Site Name: _____ http://_____
User Name: _____ Email: _____
Password: _____ Phone: _____
Acct. #: _____
Email Log In: _____
Security Questions: _____
_____
Reminders: _____
_____

Tt

Site Name: _____ http://_____
User Name: _____ Email: _____
Password: _____ Phone: _____
                                     Acct. #: _____

Email Log In: _____
Security Questions: _____
_____

Reminders: _____
_____

Site Name: _____ http://_____
User Name: _____ Email: _____
Password: _____ Phone: _____
                                     Acct. #: _____

Email Log In: _____
Security Questions: _____
_____

Reminders: _____
_____

Site Name: _____ http://_____
User Name: _____ Email: _____
Password: _____ Phone: _____
                                     Acct. #: _____

Email Log In: _____
Security Questions: _____
_____

Reminders: _____
_____

Site Name: _____ http://_____
User Name: _____ Email: _____
Password: _____ Phone: _____
                                     Acct. #: _____

Email Log In: _____
Security Questions: _____
_____

Reminders: _____
_____

Site Name: _____ http://_____
User Name: _____ Email: _____
Password: _____ Phone: _____
                                     Acct. #: _____

Email Log In: _____
Security Questions: _____
_____

Reminders: _____
_____

Tt

Site Name: _____ http://_____
User Name: _____ Email: _____
Password: _____ Phone: _____
                                   Acct. #: _____
Email Log In: _____
Security Questions: _____
_____

Reminders: _____
_____

Site Name: _____ http://_____
User Name: _____ Email: _____
Password: _____ Phone: _____
                                   Acct. #: _____
Email Log In: _____
Security Questions: _____
_____

Reminders: _____
_____

Site Name: _____ http://_____
User Name: _____ Email: _____
Password: _____ Phone: _____
                                   Acct. #: _____
Email Log In: _____
Security Questions: _____
_____

Reminders: _____
_____

Site Name: _____ http://_____
User Name: _____ Email: _____
Password: _____ Phone: _____
                                   Acct. #: _____
Email Log In: _____
Security Questions: _____
_____

Reminders: _____
_____

Site Name: _____ http://_____
User Name: _____ Email: _____
Password: _____ Phone: _____
                                   Acct. #: _____
Email Log In: _____
Security Questions: _____
_____

Reminders: _____
_____

Tt

Site Name: _____ http://_____
User Name: _____ Email: _____
Password: _____ Phone: _____
                                      Acct. #: _____
Email Log In: _____
Security Questions: _____
_____

Reminders: _____
_____

Site Name: _____ http://_____
User Name: _____ Email: _____
Password: _____ Phone: _____
                                      Acct. #: _____
Email Log In: _____
Security Questions: _____
_____

Reminders: _____
_____

Site Name: _____ http://_____
User Name: _____ Email: _____
Password: _____ Phone: _____
                                      Acct. #: _____
Email Log In: _____
Security Questions: _____
_____

Reminders: _____
_____

Site Name: _____ http://_____
User Name: _____ Email: _____
Password: _____ Phone: _____
                                      Acct. #: _____
Email Log In: _____
Security Questions: _____
_____

Reminders: _____
_____

Site Name: _____ http://_____
User Name: _____ Email: _____
Password: _____ Phone: _____
                                      Acct. #: _____
Email Log In: _____
Security Questions: _____
_____

Reminders: _____
_____

Uu

Site Name: _____ http://_____
User Name: _____ Email: _____
Password: _____ Phone: _____
Acct. #: _____

Email Log In: _____
Security Questions: _____
_____

Reminders: _____
_____

Site Name: _____ http://_____
User Name: _____ Email: _____
Password: _____ Phone: _____
Acct. #: _____

Email Log In: _____
Security Questions: _____
_____

Reminders: _____
_____

Site Name: _____ http://_____
User Name: _____ Email: _____
Password: _____ Phone: _____
Acct. #: _____

Email Log In: _____
Security Questions: _____
_____

Reminders: _____
_____

Site Name: _____ http://_____
User Name: _____ Email: _____
Password: _____ Phone: _____
Acct. #: _____

Email Log In: _____
Security Questions: _____
_____

Reminders: _____
_____

Site Name: _____ http://_____
User Name: _____ Email: _____
Password: _____ Phone: _____
Acct. #: _____

Email Log In: _____
Security Questions: _____
_____

Reminders: _____
_____

Uu

Site Name: _____ http://_____
User Name: _____ Email: _____
Password: _____ Phone: _____
                                                 Acct. #: _____
Email Log In: _____
Security Questions: _____
_____

Reminders: _____
_____

Site Name: _____ http://_____
User Name: _____ Email: _____
Password: _____ Phone: _____
                                                 Acct. #: _____
Email Log In: _____
Security Questions: _____
_____

Reminders: _____
_____

Site Name: _____ http://_____
User Name: _____ Email: _____
Password: _____ Phone: _____
                                                 Acct. #: _____
Email Log In: _____
Security Questions: _____
_____

Reminders: _____
_____

Site Name: _____ http://_____
User Name: _____ Email: _____
Password: _____ Phone: _____
                                                 Acct. #: _____
Email Log In: _____
Security Questions: _____
_____

Reminders: _____
_____

Site Name: _____ http://_____
User Name: _____ Email: _____
Password: _____ Phone: _____
                                                 Acct. #: _____
Email Log In: _____
Security Questions: _____
_____

Reminders: _____
_____

Vv

Site Name: _____ http://_____
User Name: _____ Email: _____
Password: _____ Phone: _____
Acct. #: _____
Email Log In: _____
Security Questions: _____
_____
Reminders: _____
_____

Site Name: _____ http://_____
User Name: _____ Email: _____
Password: _____ Phone: _____
Acct. #: _____
Email Log In: _____
Security Questions: _____
_____
Reminders: _____
_____

Site Name: _____ http://_____
User Name: _____ Email: _____
Password: _____ Phone: _____
Acct. #: _____
Email Log In: _____
Security Questions: _____
_____
Reminders: _____
_____

Site Name: _____ http://_____
User Name: _____ Email: _____
Password: _____ Phone: _____
Acct. #: _____
Email Log In: _____
Security Questions: _____
_____
Reminders: _____
_____

Site Name: _____ http://_____
User Name: _____ Email: _____
Password: _____ Phone: _____
Acct. #: _____
Email Log In: _____
Security Questions: _____
_____
Reminders: _____
_____

Vv

Site Name: _____ http://_____
User Name: _____ Email: _____
Password: _____ Phone: _____
                                   Acct. #: _____
Email Log In: _____
Security Questions: _____
_____
Reminders: _____
_____

Site Name: _____ http://_____
User Name: _____ Email: _____
Password: _____ Phone: _____
                                   Acct. #: _____
Email Log In: _____
Security Questions: _____
_____
Reminders: _____
_____

Site Name: _____ http://_____
User Name: _____ Email: _____
Password: _____ Phone: _____
                                   Acct. #: _____
Email Log In: _____
Security Questions: _____
_____
Reminders: _____
_____

Site Name: _____ http://_____
User Name: _____ Email: _____
Password: _____ Phone: _____
                                   Acct. #: _____
Email Log In: _____
Security Questions: _____
_____
Reminders: _____
_____

Site Name: _____ http://_____
User Name: _____ Email: _____
Password: _____ Phone: _____
                                   Acct. #: _____
Email Log In: _____
Security Questions: _____
_____
Reminders: _____
_____

Site Name: _____ http://_____
User Name: _____ Email: _____
Password: _____ Phone: _____
Acct. #: _____
Email Log In: _____
Security Questions: _____
_____

Reminders: _____
_____

Site Name: _____ http://_____
User Name: _____ Email: _____
Password: _____ Phone: _____
Acct. #: _____
Email Log In: _____
Security Questions: _____
_____

Reminders: _____
_____

Site Name: _____ http://_____
User Name: _____ Email: _____
Password: _____ Phone: _____
Acct. #: _____
Email Log In: _____
Security Questions: _____
_____

Reminders: _____
_____

Site Name: _____ http://_____
User Name: _____ Email: _____
Password: _____ Phone: _____
Acct. #: _____
Email Log In: _____
Security Questions: _____
_____

Reminders: _____
_____

Site Name: _____ http://_____
User Name: _____ Email: _____
Password: _____ Phone: _____
Acct. #: _____
Email Log In: _____
Security Questions: _____
_____

Reminders: _____
_____

Ww

Site Name: _____ http://_____
User Name: _____ Email: _____
Password: _____ Phone: _____
                                               Acct. #: _____
Email Log In: _____
Security Questions: _____
_____
Reminders: _____
_____

Site Name: _____ http://_____
User Name: _____ Email: _____
Password: _____ Phone: _____
                                               Acct. #: _____
Email Log In: _____
Security Questions: _____
_____
Reminders: _____
_____

Site Name: _____ http://_____
User Name: _____ Email: _____
Password: _____ Phone: _____
                                               Acct. #: _____
Email Log In: _____
Security Questions: _____
_____
Reminders: _____
_____

Site Name: _____ http://_____
User Name: _____ Email: _____
Password: _____ Phone: _____
                                               Acct. #: _____
Email Log In: _____
Security Questions: _____
_____
Reminders: _____
_____

Site Name: _____ http://_____
User Name: _____ Email: _____
Password: _____ Phone: _____
                                               Acct. #: _____
Email Log In: _____
Security Questions: _____
_____
Reminders: _____
_____

Site Name: _____ http://_____

User Name: _____ Email: _____

Password: _____ Phone: _____

Acct. #: _____

Email Log In: _____

Security Questions: _____

_____

Reminders: _____

_____

Site Name: _____ http://_____

User Name: _____ Email: _____

Password: _____ Phone: _____

Acct. #: _____

Email Log In: _____

Security Questions: _____

_____

Reminders: _____

_____

Site Name: _____ http://_____

User Name: _____ Email: _____

Password: _____ Phone: _____

Acct. #: _____

Email Log In: _____

Security Questions: _____

_____

Reminders: _____

_____

Site Name: _____ http://_____

User Name: _____ Email: _____

Password: _____ Phone: _____

Acct. #: _____

Email Log In: _____

Security Questions: _____

_____

Reminders: _____

_____

Site Name: _____ http://_____

User Name: _____ Email: _____

Password: _____ Phone: _____

Acct. #: _____

Email Log In: _____

Security Questions: _____

_____

Reminders: _____

_____

Ww

Site Name: _____ http://_____
User Name: _____ Email: _____
Password: _____ Phone: _____
                                        Acct. #: _____
Email Log In: _____
Security Questions: _____
_____
Reminders: _____
_____

Site Name: _____ http://_____
User Name: _____ Email: _____
Password: _____ Phone: _____
                                        Acct. #: _____
Email Log In: _____
Security Questions: _____
_____
Reminders: _____
_____

Site Name: _____ http://_____
User Name: _____ Email: _____
Password: _____ Phone: _____
                                        Acct. #: _____
Email Log In: _____
Security Questions: _____
_____
Reminders: _____
_____

Site Name: _____ http://_____
User Name: _____ Email: _____
Password: _____ Phone: _____
                                        Acct. #: _____
Email Log In: _____
Security Questions: _____
_____
Reminders: _____
_____

Site Name: _____ http://_____
User Name: _____ Email: _____
Password: _____ Phone: _____
                                        Acct. #: _____
Email Log In: _____
Security Questions: _____
_____
Reminders: _____
_____

XxYyZz

Site Name: _____ http://_____
User Name: _____ Email: _____
Password: _____ Phone: _____
Acct. #: _____

Email Log In: _____
Security Questions: _____
_____

Reminders: _____
_____

Site Name: _____ http://_____
User Name: _____ Email: _____
Password: _____ Phone: _____
Acct. #: _____

Email Log In: _____
Security Questions: _____
_____

Reminders: _____
_____

Site Name: _____ http://_____
User Name: _____ Email: _____
Password: _____ Phone: _____
Acct. #: _____

Email Log In: _____
Security Questions: _____
_____

Reminders: _____
_____

Site Name: _____ http://_____
User Name: _____ Email: _____
Password: _____ Phone: _____
Acct. #: _____

Email Log In: _____
Security Questions: _____
_____

Reminders: _____
_____

Site Name: _____ http://_____
User Name: _____ Email: _____
Password: _____ Phone: _____
Acct. #: _____

Email Log In: _____
Security Questions: _____
_____

Reminders: _____
_____

XxYyZz

Site Name: _____ http://_____
User Name: _____ Email: _____
Password: _____ Phone: _____
_____ Acct. #: _____

Email Log In: _____
Security Questions: _____
_____

Reminders: _____
_____

Site Name: _____ http://_____
User Name: _____ Email: _____
Password: _____ Phone: _____
_____ Acct. #: _____

Email Log In: _____
Security Questions: _____
_____

Reminders: _____
_____

Site Name: _____ http://_____
User Name: _____ Email: _____
Password: _____ Phone: _____
_____ Acct. #: _____

Email Log In: _____
Security Questions: _____
_____

Reminders: _____
_____

Site Name: _____ http://_____
User Name: _____ Email: _____
Password: _____ Phone: _____
_____ Acct. #: _____

Email Log In: _____
Security Questions: _____
_____

Reminders: _____
_____

Site Name: _____ http://_____
User Name: _____ Email: _____
Password: _____ Phone: _____
_____ Acct. #: _____

Email Log In: _____
Security Questions: _____
_____

Reminders: _____
_____

Log

Log

Log

Log

Log

Log

Social Media Notes/Contacts

Social Media Notes/Contacts

Social Media Notes/Contacts

Social Media Notes/Contacts

www.ingramcontent.com/pod-product-compliance
Lightning Source LLC
Chambersburg PA
CBHW060948050326
40689CB00012B/2596